Contacts and T

MW01173295

PANTHERIA™

LIFE LOG

Life Building Tool for Work,
Self-Improvement, Goals,
or Anything else

Copyright 2021 @ **Panterax Ltd**
All Rights Reserved.

All rights reserved. No part of this publications may be
reproduced, distributed, or transmitted in any form or by
any means, including photocopying, recording, other
electronic, or mechanical methods.

The Story So Far...

My Name is _____ Today is _____

I am _____ at _____
       (Title or Profession)   (Company, Team, Unit)

My Goal in life is _____
                     (Big Goal or Vision you want before you die)

To get there I must (List some Major Milestones)

_____

_____

_____

_____

So Far I have (List Some Accomplishments)

_____

_____

_____

_____

For now, I must (List major obstacles or requirements)

_____

_____

_____

EVERYDAY, with EVERY PAGE,
I move closer to My Dream........

THINGS I'M GRATEFUL FOR

1. _____
2. _____
3. _____

VITALS

WEIGHT	BLOOD PRESSURE	HEART RATE

TODAYS EVENTS

_____
_____
_____
_____
_____
_____
_____
_____
_____
_____
_____
_____
_____
_____
_____
_____
_____

TODAY GOALS

- ☐ _____
- ☐ _____
- ☐ _____
- ☐ _____

TASK AND NOTES

....
....
....
....
....
....
....
....
....
....
....
....
....
....

TODAYS WINS

....
....
....

TODAYS LESSONS

....
....
....

MY LOCATION

MEAL

Breakfast	Lunch
Dinner	Snack

WATER INTAKE
◇ ◇ ◇ ◇ ◇ ◇ ◇ ◇

DAILY EXERCISE

TODAY I FEEL

ADDITIONAL NOTES

(Thoughts, Reflections)

DATE ⟨_____⟩   Ⓢ Ⓜ Ⓣ Ⓦ Ⓣ Ⓕ Ⓢ

THINGS I'M GRATEFUL FOR

1. _____
2. _____
3. _____

VITALS

WEIGHT	BLOOD PRESSURE	HEART RATE

TODAYS EVENTS

_____
_____
_____
_____
_____
_____
_____
_____
_____
_____
_____
_____
_____
_____
_____

TODAY GOALS

☐ _____
☐ _____
☐ _____
☐ _____

TASK AND NOTES

....
....
....
....
....
....
....
....
....
....
....
....
....
....

TODAYS WINS

....
....
....

MY LOCATION

TODAYS LESSONS

....
....
....

MEAL

Breakfast	Lunch
Dinner	Snack

WATER INTAKE
◇ ◇ ◇ ◇ ◇ ◇ ◇ ◇

DAILY EXERCISE

TODAY I FEEL   😊 😌 😳 😣 🙁

ADDITIONAL NOTES
(Thoughts, Reflections)

DATE

THINGS I'M GRATEFUL FOR

1. _____
2. _____
3. _____

VITALS

WEIGHT	BLOOD PRESSURE	HEART RATE

TODAYS EVENTS

_____
_____
_____
_____
_____
_____
_____
_____
_____
_____
_____
_____
_____
_____
_____
_____
_____
_____
_____

TODAY GOALS

- ☐ _____
- ☐ _____
- ☐ _____
- ☐ _____

TASK AND NOTES

....
....
....
....
....
....
....
....
....
....
....
....
....
....

TODAYS WINS

....
....
....

TODAYS LESSONS

....
....
....

MY LOCATION

MEAL

Breakfast	Lunch
Dinner	Snack

WATER INTAKE

DAILY EXERCISE

TODAY I FEEL

ADDITIONAL NOTES

(Thoughts, Reflections)

DATE

⟨S⟩ ⟨M⟩ ⟨T⟩ ⟨W⟩ ⟨T⟩ ⟨F⟩ ⟨S⟩

THINGS I'M GRATEFUL FOR

1. _____

2. _____

3. _____

VITALS

WEIGHT	BLOOD PRESSURE	HEART RATE

TODAYS EVENTS

_____
_____
_____
_____
_____
_____
_____
_____
_____
_____
_____
_____
_____
_____
_____
_____
_____

TODAY GOALS

☐ _____
☐ _____
☐ _____
☐ _____

TASK AND NOTES

....
....
....
....
....
....
....
....
....
....
....
....
....
....

TODAYS WINS

....
....
....

TODAYS LESSONS

....
....
....

MY LOCATION

MEAL

Breakfast	Lunch
Dinner	Snack

WATER INTAKE

DAILY EXERCISE

TODAY I FEEL

ADDITIONAL NOTES
(Thoughts, Reflections)

DATE ⬭

Ⓢ Ⓜ Ⓣ Ⓦ Ⓣ Ⓕ Ⓢ

THINGS I'M GRATEFUL FOR

1. _____
2. _____
3. _____

VITALS

WEIGHT	BLOOD PRESSURE	HEART RATE

TODAYS EVENTS

_____
_____
_____
_____
_____
_____
_____
_____
_____
_____
_____
_____
_____
_____
_____
_____
_____

TODAY GOALS

☐ _____
☐ _____
☐ _____
☐ _____

TASK AND NOTES

....
....
....
....
....
....
....
....
....
....
....
....
....

TODAYS WINS
....
....
....

MY LOCATION

TODAYS LESSONS
....
....
....

MEAL

Breakfast	Lunch
Dinner	Snack

WATER INTAKE
🝆 🝆 🝆 🝆 🝆 🝆 🝆 🝆

DAILY EXERCISE

TODAY I FEEL

ADDITIONAL NOTES
(Thoughts, Reflections)

DATE ⬭ Ⓢ Ⓜ Ⓣ Ⓦ Ⓣ Ⓕ Ⓢ

THINGS I'M GRATEFUL FOR

1. _____
2. _____
3. _____

VITALS

WEIGHT	BLOOD PRESSURE	HEART RATE

TODAYS EVENTS

_____
_____
_____
_____
_____
_____
_____
_____
_____
_____
_____
_____
_____
_____
_____
_____
_____
_____

TODAY GOALS

☐ _____
☐ _____
☐ _____
☐ _____

TASK AND NOTES

....
....
....
....
....
....
....
....
....
....
....
....
....
....

TODAYS WINS

....
....
....

TODAYS LESSONS

....
....
....

MY LOCATION

MEAL

Breakfast	Lunch
Dinner	Snack

WATER INTAKE
◇◇◇◇◇◇◇◇

DAILY EXERCISE

TODAY I FEEL   😊   😌   😳   😠   😟

ADDITIONAL NOTES
(Thoughts, Reflections)

DATE ( )

$(S)(M)(T)(W)(T)(F)(S)$

THINGS I'M GRATEFUL FOR

1. _____
2. _____
3. _____

VITALS

WEIGHT	BLOOD PRESSURE	HEART RATE

TODAYS EVENTS

_____
_____
_____
_____
_____
_____
_____
_____
_____
_____
_____
_____
_____
_____
_____
_____
_____
_____
_____
_____
_____

TODAY GOALS

☐ _____
☐ _____
☐ _____
☐ _____

TASK AND NOTES

....
....
....
....
....
....
....
....
....
....
....
....
....
....

TODAYS WINS

....
....
....

TODAYS LESSONS

....
....
....

MY LOCATION

MEAL

Breakfast	Lunch
Dinner	Snack

WATER INTAKE
◇◇◇◇◇◇◇◇

DAILY EXERCISE

TODAY I FEEL

ADDITIONAL NOTES

(Thoughts, Reflections)

DATE _____   (S) (M) (T) (W) (T) (F) (S)

THINGS I'M GRATEFUL FOR

1. _____
2. _____
3. _____

VITALS

WEIGHT	BLOOD PRESSURE	HEART RATE

TODAYS EVENTS

_____
_____
_____
_____
_____
_____
_____
_____
_____
_____
_____
_____
_____
_____
_____
_____
_____
_____

TODAY GOALS

☐ _____
☐ _____
☐ _____
☐ _____

TASK AND NOTES

....
....
....
....
....
....
....
....
....
....
....
....
....
....

TODAYS WINS

....
....
....

TODAYS LESSONS

....
....
....

MY LOCATION

MEAL

Breakfast	Lunch
Dinner	Snack

WATER INTAKE   **DAILY EXERCISE**

◇ ◇ ◇ ◇ ◇ ◇ ◇

TODAY I FEEL

ADDITIONAL NOTES

(Thoughts, Reflections)

DATE ⬭ (S) (M) (T) (W) (T) (F) (S)

THINGS I'M GRATEFUL FOR

1. _____
2. _____
3. _____

VITALS

WEIGHT	BLOOD PRESSURE	HEART RATE

TODAYS EVENTS

_____
_____
_____
_____
_____
_____
_____
_____
_____
_____
_____
_____
_____
_____
_____
_____
_____
_____
_____
_____
_____

TODAY GOALS

☐ _____
☐ _____
☐ _____
☐ _____

TASK AND NOTES

....
....
....
....
....
....
....
....
....
....
....
....
....
....

TODAYS WINS

....
....
....

TODAYS LESSONS

....
....
....

MY LOCATION

MEAL

Breakfast	Lunch
Dinner	Snack

WATER INTAKE
◌ ◌ ◌ ◌ ◌ ◌ ◌ ◌

DAILY EXERCISE

TODAY I FEEL

ADDITIONAL NOTES

(Thoughts, Reflections)

DATE ⟨ ⟩   (S) (M) (T) (W) (T) (F) (S)

THINGS I'M GRATEFUL FOR

1. _____
2. _____
3. _____

VITALS

WEIGHT	BLOOD PRESSURE	HEART RATE

TODAYS EVENTS

_____
_____
_____
_____
_____
_____
_____
_____
_____
_____
_____
_____
_____
_____
_____
_____
_____
_____

TODAY GOALS

- [ ] _____
- [ ] _____
- [ ] _____
- [ ] _____

TASK AND NOTES

....
....
....
....
....
....
....
....
....
....
....
....
....
....
....

TODAYS WINS

....
....
....

TODAYS LESSONS

....
....
....

MY LOCATION

MEAL

Breakfast	Lunch
Dinner	Snack

WATER INTAKE

DAILY EXERCISE

TODAY I FEEL

ADDITIONAL NOTES

(Thoughts, Reflections)

DATE ⬭

(S) (M) (T) (W) (T) (F) (S)

THINGS I'M GRATEFUL FOR

1. _____
2. _____
3. _____

VITALS

WEIGHT	BLOOD PRESSURE	HEART RATE

TODAYS EVENTS

_____
_____
_____
_____
_____
_____
_____
_____
_____
_____
_____
_____
_____
_____
_____
_____
_____
_____
_____
_____

TODAY GOALS

☐ _____
☐ _____
☐ _____
☐ _____

TASK AND NOTES

....
....
....
....
....
....
....
....
....
....
....
....
....
....

TODAYS WINS

....
....
....

MY LOCATION

TODAYS LESSONS

....
....
....

MEAL

Breakfast	Lunch
Dinner	Snack

WATER INTAKE
◇◇◇◇◇◇◇◇

DAILY EXERCISE

TODAY I FEEL

ADDITIONAL NOTES

(Thoughts, Reflections)

DATE (⬭)   (S) (M) (T) (W) (T) (F) (S)

THINGS I'M GRATEFUL FOR

1. _____
2. _____
3. _____

VITALS

WEIGHT	BLOOD PRESSURE	HEART RATE

TODAYS EVENTS

_____
_____
_____
_____
_____
_____
_____
_____
_____
_____
_____
_____
_____
_____
_____
_____
_____
_____

TODAY GOALS

☐ _____
☐ _____
☐ _____
☐ _____

TASK AND NOTES

....
....
....
....
....
....
....
....
....
....
....
....
....

TODAYS WINS
....
....
....

MY LOCATION

TODAYS LESSONS
....
....
....

MEAL

Breakfast	Lunch
Dinner	Snack

WATER INTAKE
🜄 🜄 🜄 🜄 🜄 🜄 🜄 🜄

DAILY EXERCISE

TODAY I FEEL (😊) (😌) (😐) (😠) (😟)

ADDITIONAL NOTES
(Thoughts, Reflections)

DATE [_____]   Ⓢ Ⓜ Ⓣ Ⓦ Ⓣ Ⓕ Ⓢ

THINGS I'M GRATEFUL FOR

1. _____

2. _____

3. _____

VITALS

WEIGHT	BLOOD PRESSURE	HEART RATE

TODAYS EVENTS

_____
_____
_____
_____
_____
_____
_____
_____
_____
_____
_____
_____
_____
_____
_____

TODAY GOALS

☐ _____
☐ _____
☐ _____
☐ _____

TASK AND NOTES

....
....
....
....
....
....
....
....
....
....
....
....
....

TODAYS WINS

....
....
....

TODAYS LESSONS

....
....
....

MY LOCATION

[_____]

MEAL

Breakfast	Lunch
Dinner	Snack

WATER INTAKE
◌◌◌◌◌◌◌◌

DAILY EXERCISE
[_____]

TODAY I FEEL

ADDITIONAL NOTES

(Thoughts, Reflections)

DATE ⬭

(S)(M)(T)(W)(T)(F)(S)

THINGS I'M GRATEFUL FOR

1. _____
2. _____
3. _____

VITALS

WEIGHT	BLOOD PRESSURE	HEART RATE

TODAYS EVENTS

_____
_____
_____
_____
_____
_____
_____
_____
_____
_____
_____
_____
_____
_____
_____
_____
_____

TODAY GOALS

☐ _____
☐ _____
☐ _____
☐ _____

TASK AND NOTES

....
....
....
....
....
....
....
....
....
....
....
....
....
....
....
....

TODAYS WINS

....
....
....

MY LOCATION

TODAYS LESSONS

....
....
....

MEAL

Breakfast	Lunch
Dinner	Snack

WATER INTAKE
◇◇◇◇◇◇◇◇

DAILY EXERCISE

TODAY I FEEL

ADDITIONAL NOTES
(Thoughts, Reflections)

DATE ⬭

S M T W T F S

THINGS I'M GRATEFUL FOR

1. _____
2. _____
3. _____

VITALS

WEIGHT	BLOOD PRESSURE	HEART RATE

TODAYS EVENTS

_____
_____
_____
_____
_____
_____
_____
_____
_____
_____
_____
_____
_____
_____
_____
_____
_____
_____
_____
_____
_____

TODAY GOALS

☐ _____
☐ _____
☐ _____
☐ _____

TASK AND NOTES

....
....
....
....
....
....
....
....
....
....
....
....
....

TODAYS WINS

....
....
....

TODAYS LESSONS

....
....
....

MY LOCATION

_____

MEAL

| Breakfast | Lunch |
| Dinner | Snack |

WATER INTAKE
◇◇◇◇◇◇◇◇

DAILY EXERCISE
_____

TODAY I FEEL

ADDITIONAL NOTES

(Thoughts, Reflections)

DATE

S M T W T F S

THINGS I'M GRATEFUL FOR

1.
2.
3.

VITALS

WEIGHT	BLOOD PRESSURE	HEART RATE

TODAYS EVENTS

TODAY GOALS

- [ ]
- [ ]
- [ ]
- [ ]

TASK AND NOTES

TODAYS WINS

MY LOCATION

MEAL

Breakfast	Lunch
Dinner	Snack

TODAYS LESSONS

WATER INTAKE

DAILY EXERCISE

TODAY I FEEL

ADDITIONAL NOTES
(Thoughts, Reflections)

DATE [_____]

(S) (M) (T) (W) (T) (F) (S)

THINGS I'M GRATEFUL FOR

1. _____
2. _____
3. _____

VITALS

WEIGHT	BLOOD PRESSURE	HEART RATE

TODAYS EVENTS

_____
_____
_____
_____
_____
_____
_____
_____
_____
_____
_____
_____
_____
_____
_____
_____
_____
_____
_____

TODAY GOALS

☐ _____
☐ _____
☐ _____
☐ _____

TASK AND NOTES

....
....
....
....
....
....
....
....
....
....
....
....
....

TODAYS WINS

....
....
....

MY LOCATION

[_____]

TODAYS LESSONS

....
....
....

MEAL

Breakfast	Lunch
Dinner	Snack

WATER INTAKE
◇ ◇ ◇ ◇ ◇ ◇ ◇ ◇

DAILY EXERCISE
[_____]

TODAY I FEEL

ADDITIONAL NOTES

(Thoughts, Reflections)

DATE ⬭   (S)(M)(T)(W)(T)(F)(S)

THINGS I'M GRATEFUL FOR

1. _____
2. _____
3. _____

VITALS

WEIGHT	BLOOD PRESSURE	HEART RATE

TODAYS EVENTS

_____
_____
_____
_____
_____
_____
_____
_____
_____
_____
_____
_____
_____
_____
_____
_____
_____

TODAY GOALS

☐ _____
☐ _____
☐ _____
☐ _____

TASK AND NOTES

....
....
....
....
....
....
....
....
....
....
....
....
....

TODAYS WINS
....
....
....

TODAYS LESSONS
....
....
....

MY LOCATION

MEAL

Breakfast	Lunch
Dinner	Snack

WATER INTAKE
◇◇◇◇◇◇◇◇

DAILY EXERCISE

TODAY I FEEL

ADDITIONAL NOTES
(Thoughts, Reflections)

DATE ⬭

(S) (M) (T) (W) (T) (F) (S)

THINGS I'M GRATEFUL FOR

1. _____
2. _____
3. _____

VITALS

WEIGHT	BLOOD PRESSURE	HEART RATE

TODAYS EVENTS

_____
_____
_____
_____
_____
_____
_____
_____
_____
_____
_____
_____
_____
_____
_____

TODAY GOALS

☐ _____
☐ _____
☐ _____
☐ _____

TASK AND NOTES

....
....
....
....
....
....
....
....
....
....
....
....
....
....

TODAYS WINS

....
....
....

TODAYS LESSONS

....
....
....

MY LOCATION

MEAL

| Breakfast | | Lunch |
| Dinner | | Snack |

WATER INTAKE
◇◇◇◇◇◇◇◇

DAILY EXERCISE

TODAY I FEEL

ADDITIONAL NOTES

(Thoughts, Reflections)

DATE ⬭   (S) (M) (T) (W) (T) (F) (S)

THINGS I'M GRATEFUL FOR

1. _____
2. _____
3. _____

VITALS

WEIGHT	BLOOD PRESSURE	HEART RATE

TODAYS EVENTS

_____
_____
_____
_____
_____
_____
_____
_____
_____
_____
_____
_____
_____
_____
_____
_____
_____
_____
_____

TODAY GOALS

- ☐ _____
- ☐ _____
- ☐ _____
- ☐ _____

TASK AND NOTES

....
....
....
....
....
....
....
....
....
....
....
....
....
....

TODAYS WINS

....
....
....

TODAYS LESSONS

....
....
....

MY LOCATION

MEAL

Breakfast	Lunch
Dinner	Snack

WATER INTAKE
◇◇◇◇◇◇◇◇

DAILY EXERCISE

TODAY I FEEL

ADDITIONAL NOTES

(Thoughts, Reflections)

DATE ⬭

Ⓢ Ⓜ Ⓣ Ⓦ Ⓣ Ⓕ Ⓢ

THINGS I'M GRATEFUL FOR

1. _____
2. _____
3. _____

VITALS

WEIGHT	BLOOD PRESSURE	HEART RATE

TODAYS EVENTS

_____
_____
_____
_____
_____
_____
_____
_____
_____
_____
_____
_____
_____
_____
_____
_____
_____

TODAY GOALS

- ☐ _____
- ☐ _____
- ☐ _____
- ☐ _____

TASK AND NOTES

....
....
....
....
....
....
....
....
....
....
....
....
....
....
....

TODAYS WINS

....
....
....

MY LOCATION

TODAYS LESSONS

....
....
....

MEAL

Breakfast	Lunch
Dinner	Snack

WATER INTAKE
◇◇◇◇◇◇◇◇

DAILY EXERCISE

TODAY I FEEL

ADDITIONAL NOTES

(Thoughts, Reflections)

DATE [   ] Ⓢ Ⓜ Ⓣ Ⓦ Ⓣ Ⓕ Ⓢ

THINGS I'M GRATEFUL FOR

1. _____
2. _____
3. _____

VITALS

WEIGHT	BLOOD PRESSURE	HEART RATE

TODAYS EVENTS

_____
_____
_____
_____
_____
_____
_____
_____
_____
_____
_____
_____
_____
_____
_____
_____
_____
_____
_____

TODAY GOALS

☐ _____
☐ _____
☐ _____
☐ _____

TASK AND NOTES

....
....
....
....
....
....
....
....
....
....
....
....
....
....
....

TODAYS WINS

....
....
....

TODAYS LESSONS

....
....
....

MY LOCATION

[   ]

MEAL

Breakfast	Lunch
Dinner	Snack

WATER INTAKE
◌ ◌ ◌ ◌ ◌ ◌ ◌ ◌

DAILY EXERCISE
[   ]

TODAY I FEEL

ADDITIONAL NOTES

(Thoughts, Reflections)

DATE ⬭ Ⓢ Ⓜ Ⓣ Ⓦ Ⓣ Ⓕ Ⓢ

THINGS I'M GRATEFUL FOR

1. _____

2. _____

3. _____

VITALS

WEIGHT	BLOOD PRESSURE	HEART RATE

TODAYS EVENTS

_____
_____
_____
_____
_____
_____
_____
_____
_____
_____
_____
_____
_____
_____
_____
_____

TODAY GOALS

☐ _____
☐ _____
☐ _____
☐ _____

TASK AND NOTES

....
....
....
....
....
....
....
....
....
....
....
....
....
....

TODAYS WINS

....
....
....

TODAYS LESSONS

....
....
....

MY LOCATION

_____

MEAL

Breakfast	Lunch
Dinner	Snack

WATER INTAKE
⬙ ⬙ ⬙ ⬙ ⬙ ⬙ ⬙ ⬙

DAILY EXERCISE
_____

TODAY I FEEL

ADDITIONAL NOTES

(Thoughts, Reflections)

DATE

THINGS I'M GRATEFUL FOR

1. _____
2. _____
3. _____

VITALS

WEIGHT	BLOOD PRESSURE	HEART RATE

TODAYS EVENTS

_____
_____
_____
_____
_____
_____
_____
_____
_____
_____
_____
_____
_____
_____
_____
_____
_____
_____
_____
_____
_____

TODAY GOALS

- [ ] _____
- [ ] _____
- [ ] _____
- [ ] _____

TASK AND NOTES

....
....
....
....
....
....
....
....
....
....
....
....
....
....

TODAYS WINS

....
....
....

TODAYS LESSONS

....
....
....

MY LOCATION

MEAL

Breakfast	Lunch
Dinner	Snack

WATER INTAKE

DAILY EXERCISE

TODAY I FEEL

ADDITIONAL NOTES

(Thoughts, Reflections)

DATE ⬭

Ⓢ Ⓜ Ⓣ Ⓦ Ⓣ Ⓕ Ⓢ

THINGS I'M GRATEFUL FOR

1. _____

2. _____

3. _____

VITALS

WEIGHT	BLOOD PRESSURE	HEART RATE

TODAYS EVENTS

_____
_____
_____
_____
_____
_____
_____
_____
_____
_____
_____
_____
_____
_____
_____

TODAY GOALS

☐ _____
☐ _____
☐ _____
☐ _____

TASK AND NOTES

....
....
....
....
....
....
....
....
....
....
....
....
....
....

TODAYS WINS

....
....
....

TODAYS LESSONS

....
....
....

MY LOCATION

MEAL

Breakfast	Lunch
Dinner	Snack

WATER INTAKE
◇ ◇ ◇ ◇ ◇ ◇ ◇ ◇

DAILY EXERCISE

TODAY I FEEL

ADDITIONAL NOTES
(Thoughts, Reflections)

DATE ⟨ ⟩

(S) (M) (T) (W) (T) (F) (S)

THINGS I'M GRATEFUL FOR

1. _____
2. _____
3. _____

VITALS

WEIGHT	BLOOD PRESSURE	HEART RATE

TODAYS EVENTS

_____
_____
_____
_____
_____
_____
_____
_____
_____
_____
_____
_____
_____
_____
_____
_____
_____
_____

TODAY GOALS

☐ _____
☐ _____
☐ _____
☐ _____

TASK AND NOTES

....
....
....
....
....
....
....
....
....
....
....
....
....
....

TODAYS WINS

....
....
....

TODAYS LESSONS

....
....
....

MY LOCATION

MEAL

Breakfast	Lunch
Dinner	Snack

WATER INTAKE
◇◇◇◇◇◇◇◇

DAILY EXERCISE

TODAY I FEEL

ADDITIONAL NOTES

(Thoughts, Reflections)

DATE ⟨_____⟩ Ⓢ Ⓜ Ⓣ Ⓦ Ⓣ Ⓕ Ⓢ

THINGS I'M GRATEFUL FOR

1. _____
2. _____
3. _____

VITALS

WEIGHT	BLOOD PRESSURE	HEART RATE

TODAYS EVENTS

_____
_____
_____
_____
_____
_____
_____
_____
_____
_____
_____
_____
_____
_____
_____
_____
_____
_____

TODAY GOALS

☐ _____
☐ _____
☐ _____
☐ _____

TASK AND NOTES

....
....
....
....
....
....
....
....
....
....
....
....
....

TODAYS WINS
....
....
....

TODAYS LESSONS
....
....
....

MY LOCATION

_____

MEAL

Breakfast | Lunch

Dinner | Snack

WATER INTAKE
◇ ◇ ◇ ◇ ◇ ◇ ◇ ◇

DAILY EXERCISE
_____

TODAY I FEEL

ADDITIONAL NOTES

(Thoughts, Reflections)

DATE ⬭

(S) (M) (T) (W) (T) (F) (S)

THINGS I'M GRATEFUL FOR

1. _____
2. _____
3. _____

VITALS

WEIGHT	BLOOD PRESSURE	HEART RATE

TODAYS EVENTS

_____
_____
_____
_____
_____
_____
_____
_____
_____
_____
_____
_____
_____
_____
_____
_____
_____
_____

TODAY GOALS

- ☐ _____
- ☐ _____
- ☐ _____
- ☐ _____

TASK AND NOTES

....
....
....
....
....
....
....
....
....
....
....
....
....

TODAYS WINS

....
....
....

MY LOCATION

MEAL

Breakfast | Lunch

Dinner | Snack

TODAYS LESSONS

....
....
....

WATER INTAKE
◇◇◇◇◇◇◇

DAILY EXERCISE

TODAY I FEEL 😊 😌 😳 😠 😞

ADDITIONAL NOTES

(Thoughts, Reflections)

DATE _____  (S) (M) (T) (W) (T) (F) (S)

THINGS I'M GRATEFUL FOR

1. _____
2. _____
3. _____

VITALS

WEIGHT	BLOOD PRESSURE	HEART RATE

TODAYS EVENTS

_____
_____
_____
_____
_____
_____
_____
_____
_____
_____
_____
_____
_____
_____
_____

TODAY GOALS

☐ _____
☐ _____
☐ _____
☐ _____

TASK AND NOTES

....
....
....
....
....
....
....
....
....
....
....
....
....
....

TODAYS WINS

....
....
....

TODAYS LESSONS

....
....
....

MY LOCATION

MEAL

Breakfast   Lunch

Dinner   Snack

WATER INTAKE
◇◇◇◇◇◇◇◇

DAILY EXERCISE

TODAY I FEEL

ADDITIONAL NOTES
(Thoughts, Reflections)

DATE

THINGS I'M GRATEFUL FOR

1. _____

2. _____

3. _____

VITALS

WEIGHT	BLOOD PRESSURE	HEART RATE

TODAYS EVENTS

_____
_____
_____
_____
_____
_____
_____
_____
_____
_____
_____
_____
_____
_____
_____
_____
_____
_____
_____

TODAY GOALS

- ☐ _____
- ☐ _____
- ☐ _____
- ☐ _____

TASK AND NOTES

....
....
....
....
....
....
....
....
....
....
....
....
....

TODAYS WINS

....
....
....

MY LOCATION

TODAYS LESSONS

....
....
....

MEAL

Breakfast   Lunch

Dinner   Snack

WATER INTAKE
◇◇◇◇◇◇◇◇

DAILY EXERCISE

TODAY I FEEL

ADDITIONAL NOTES

(Thoughts, Reflections)

DATE

THINGS I'M GRATEFUL FOR

1.
2.
3.

VITALS

WEIGHT	BLOOD PRESSURE	HEART RATE

TODAYS EVENTS

TODAY GOALS

- [ ]
- [ ]
- [ ]
- [ ]

TASK AND NOTES

TODAYS WINS

MY LOCATION

TODAYS LESSONS

MEAL

Breakfast   Lunch

Dinner   Snack

WATER INTAKE
⬦⬦⬦⬦⬦⬦⬦⬦

DAILY EXERCISE

TODAY I FEEL

ADDITIONAL NOTES
(Thoughts, Reflections)

DATE

THINGS I'M GRATEFUL FOR

1.
2.
3.

VITALS

WEIGHT	BLOOD PRESSURE	HEART RATE

TODAYS EVENTS

TODAY GOALS

- [ ]
- [ ]
- [ ]
- [ ]

TASK AND NOTES

TODAYS WINS

MY LOCATION

MEAL

Breakfast   Lunch

Dinner   Snack

TODAYS LESSONS

WATER INTAKE

DAILY EXERCISE

TODAY I FEEL

ADDITIONAL NOTES
(Thoughts, Reflections)

DATE ⬭

(S) (M) (T) (W) (T) (F) (S)

THINGS I'M GRATEFUL FOR

1. _____
2. _____
3. _____

VITALS

WEIGHT	BLOOD PRESSURE	HEART RATE

TODAYS EVENTS

_____
_____
_____
_____
_____
_____
_____
_____
_____
_____
_____
_____
_____
_____
_____
_____
_____
_____
_____

TODAY GOALS

☐ _____
☐ _____
☐ _____
☐ _____

TASK AND NOTES

....
....
....
....
....
....
....
....
....
....
....
....
....

TODAYS WINS

....
....
....

TODAYS LESSONS

....
....
....

MY LOCATION

MEAL

Breakfast	Lunch
Dinner	Snack

WATER INTAKE
◌◌◌◌◌◌◌

DAILY EXERCISE

TODAY I FEEL   😊   😌   😐   😠   😟

ADDITIONAL NOTES

(Thoughts, Reflections)

DATE ⬭

THINGS I'M GRATEFUL FOR

1. _____
2. _____
3. _____

VITALS

WEIGHT	BLOOD PRESSURE	HEART RATE

TODAYS EVENTS

_____
_____
_____
_____
_____
_____
_____
_____
_____
_____
_____
_____
_____
_____
_____
_____
_____
_____
_____

TODAY GOALS

☐ _____
☐ _____
☐ _____
☐ _____

TASK AND NOTES

....
....
....
....
....
....
....
....
....
....
....
....
....

TODAYS WINS

....
....
....

TODAYS LESSONS

....
....
....

MY LOCATION

MEAL

Breakfast | Lunch

Dinner | Snack

WATER INTAKE
◇◇◇◇◇◇◇◇

DAILY EXERCISE

TODAY I FEEL

😊 😌 😐 😠 😟

ADDITIONAL NOTES
(Thoughts, Reflections)

DATE ( )   (S) (M) (T) (W) (T) (F) (S)

THINGS I'M GRATEFUL FOR

1. _____
2. _____
3. _____

VITALS

WEIGHT	BLOOD PRESSURE	HEART RATE

TODAYS EVENTS

_____
_____
_____
_____
_____
_____
_____
_____
_____
_____
_____
_____
_____
_____
_____
_____
_____
_____
_____

TODAY GOALS

☐ _____
☐ _____
☐ _____
☐ _____

TASK AND NOTES

....
....
....
....
....
....
....
....
....
....
....
....

TODAYS WINS

....
....
....

MY LOCATION

TODAYS LESSONS

....
....
....

MEAL

| Breakfast | Lunch |
| Dinner | Snack |

WATER INTAKE
◇◇◇◇◇◇◇◇

DAILY EXERCISE

TODAY I FEEL 😊 😌 😳 😠 😞

ADDITIONAL NOTES
(Thoughts, Reflections)

DATE [   ]

(S) (M) (T) (W) (T) (F) (S)

THINGS I'M GRATEFUL FOR

1. _____

2. _____

3. _____

VITALS

WEIGHT	BLOOD PRESSURE	HEART RATE

TODAYS EVENTS

_____
_____
_____
_____
_____
_____
_____
_____
_____
_____
_____
_____
_____
_____
_____
_____
_____

TODAY GOALS

- [ ] _____
- [ ] _____
- [ ] _____
- [ ] _____

TASK AND NOTES

....
....
....
....
....
....
....
....
....
....
....
....
....

TODAYS WINS

....
....
....

MY LOCATION

TODAYS LESSONS

....
....
....

MEAL

Breakfast   Lunch

Dinner   Snack

WATER INTAKE
◇◇◇◇◇◇◇◇

DAILY EXERCISE
[   ]

TODAY I FEEL

😊 😌 😳 😠 😣

ADDITIONAL NOTES

(Thoughts, Reflections)

DATE ⟨_____⟩   Ⓢ Ⓜ Ⓣ Ⓦ Ⓣ Ⓕ Ⓢ

THINGS I'M GRATEFUL FOR

1. _____

2. _____

3. _____

VITALS

WEIGHT	BLOOD PRESSURE	HEART RATE

TODAYS EVENTS

_____
_____
_____
_____
_____
_____
_____
_____
_____
_____
_____
_____
_____
_____
_____
_____
_____
_____
_____
_____

TODAY GOALS

☐ _____
☐ _____
☐ _____
☐ _____

TASK AND NOTES

....
....
....
....
....
....
....
....
....
....
....
....
....

TODAYS WINS

....
....
....

TODAYS LESSONS

....
....
....

MY LOCATION

MEAL

Breakfast   Lunch

Dinner   Snack

WATER INTAKE
◇◇◇◇◇◇◇

DAILY EXERCISE

TODAY I FEEL   😊 😌 😐 😣 😞

ADDITIONAL NOTES

(Thoughts, Reflections)

DATE _____

(S) (M) (T) (W) (T) (F) (S)

THINGS I'M GRATEFUL FOR

1. _____

2. _____

3. _____

VITALS

WEIGHT	BLOOD PRESSURE	HEART RATE

TODAYS EVENTS

_____
_____
_____
_____
_____
_____
_____
_____
_____
_____
_____
_____
_____
_____
_____
_____
_____
_____
_____

TODAY GOALS

- [ ] _____
- [ ] _____
- [ ] _____
- [ ] _____

TASK AND NOTES

....
....
....
....
....
....
....
....
....
....
....
....
....

TODAYS WINS

....
....
....

TODAYS LESSONS

....
....
....

MY LOCATION

MEAL

Breakfast   Lunch

Dinner   Snack

WATER INTAKE   **DAILY EXERCISE**

◊ ◊ ◊ ◊ ◊ ◊ ◊

TODAY I FEEL

ADDITIONAL NOTES

(Thoughts, Reflections)

DATE ( )

 (S) (M) (T) (W) (T) (F) (S)

THINGS I'M GRATEFUL FOR

1. _____
2. _____
3. _____

VITALS

WEIGHT	BLOOD PRESSURE	HEART RATE

TODAYS EVENTS

_____
_____
_____
_____
_____
_____
_____
_____
_____
_____
_____
_____
_____
_____
_____
_____
_____

TODAY GOALS

- ☐ _____
- ☐ _____
- ☐ _____
- ☐ _____

TASK AND NOTES

....
....
....
....
....
....
....
....
....
....
....
....
....

TODAYS WINS

....
....
....

MY LOCATION

TODAYS LESSONS

....
....
....

MEAL

Breakfast | Lunch

Dinner | Snack

WATER INTAKE

DAILY EXERCISE

TODAY I FEEL

(Thoughts, Reflections)

DATE

THINGS I'M GRATEFUL FOR

1. _____
2. _____
3. _____

VITALS

WEIGHT	BLOOD PRESSURE	HEART RATE

TODAYS EVENTS

_____
_____
_____
_____
_____
_____
_____
_____
_____
_____
_____
_____
_____
_____
_____
_____
_____
_____
_____

TODAY GOALS

- [ ] _____
- [ ] _____
- [ ] _____
- [ ] _____

TASK AND NOTES

....
....
....
....
....
....
....
....
....
....
....
....
....
....

TODAYS WINS

....
....
....

MY LOCATION

_____

MEAL

| Breakfast | Lunch |
| Dinner | Snack |

TODAYS LESSONS

....
....
....

WATER INTAKE
△ △ △ △ △ △ △

DAILY EXERCISE

TODAY I FEEL

DATE

THINGS I'M GRATEFUL FOR

1. _____
2. _____
3. _____

VITALS

WEIGHT	BLOOD PRESSURE	HEART RATE

TODAYS EVENTS

_____
_____
_____
_____
_____
_____
_____
_____
_____
_____
_____
_____
_____
_____
_____
_____
_____
_____
_____

TODAY GOALS

- [ ] _____
- [ ] _____
- [ ] _____
- [ ] _____

TASK AND NOTES

....
....
....
....
....
....
....
....
....
....
....
....

TODAYS WINS

....
....
....

MY LOCATION

TODAYS LESSONS

....
....
....

MEAL

Breakfast   Lunch

Dinner   Snack

WATER INTAKE

DAILY EXERCISE

TODAY I FEEL

ADDITIONAL NOTES

(Thoughts, Reflections)

DATE

 S M T W T F S

THINGS I'M GRATEFUL FOR

1. _____
2. _____
3. _____

VITALS

WEIGHT	BLOOD PRESSURE	HEART RATE

TODAYS EVENTS

_____
_____
_____
_____
_____
_____
_____
_____
_____
_____
_____
_____
_____
_____
_____
_____
_____
_____

TODAY GOALS

- [ ] _____
- [ ] _____
- [ ] _____
- [ ] _____

TASK AND NOTES

....
....
....
....
....
....
....
....
....
....
....
....

TODAYS WINS

....
....
....

MY LOCATION

MEAL

Breakfast	Lunch
Dinner	Snack

TODAYS LESSONS

....
....
....

WATER INTAKE
◊ ◊ ◊ ◊ ◊ ◊ ◊ ◊

DAILY EXERCISE

TODAY I FEEL

DATE ⬭

THINGS I'M GRATEFUL FOR

1. _____
2. _____
3. _____

VITALS

WEIGHT	BLOOD PRESSURE	HEART RATE

TODAYS EVENTS

_____
_____
_____
_____
_____
_____
_____
_____
_____
_____
_____
_____
_____
_____
_____
_____
_____
_____
_____

TODAY GOALS

- ☐ _____
- ☐ _____
- ☐ _____
- ☐ _____

TASK AND NOTES

....
....
....
....
....
....
....
....
....
....
....
....
....
....

TODAYS WINS

....
....
....

MY LOCATION

_____

MEAL

Breakfast | Lunch

Dinner | Snack

TODAYS LESSONS

....
....
....

WATER INTAKE
◌ ◌ ◌ ◌ ◌ ◌ ◌ ◌

DAILY EXERCISE

TODAY I FEEL

ADDITIONAL NOTES

(Thoughts, Reflections)

DATE ⬭

THINGS I'M GRATEFUL FOR

1. _____
2. _____
3. _____

VITALS

WEIGHT	BLOOD PRESSURE	HEART RATE

TODAYS EVENTS

_____
_____
_____
_____
_____
_____
_____
_____
_____
_____
_____
_____
_____
_____
_____
_____
_____
_____

TODAY GOALS

☐ _____
☐ _____
☐ _____
☐ _____

TASK AND NOTES

....
....
....
....
....
....
....
....
....
....
....
....
....

TODAYS WINS

....
....
....

TODAYS LESSONS

....
....
....

MY LOCATION

MEAL

Breakfast | Lunch

Dinner | Snack

WATER INTAKE
⬡⬡⬡⬡⬡⬡⬡⬡

DAILY EXERCISE

TODAY I FEEL

ADDITIONAL NOTES
(Thoughts, Reflections)

DATE ⬭   Ⓢ Ⓜ Ⓣ Ⓦ Ⓣ Ⓕ Ⓢ

THINGS I'M GRATEFUL FOR

1. _____
2. _____
3. _____

VITALS

WEIGHT	BLOOD PRESSURE	HEART RATE

TODAYS EVENTS

_____
_____
_____
_____
_____
_____
_____
_____
_____
_____
_____
_____
_____
_____
_____
_____
_____
_____
_____

TODAY GOALS

☐ _____
☐ _____
☐ _____
☐ _____

TASK AND NOTES

....
....
....
....
....
....
....
....
....
....
....
....
....
....

TODAYS WINS

....
....
....

TODAYS LESSONS

....
....
....

MY LOCATION

MEAL

Breakfast	Lunch
Dinner	Snack

WATER INTAKE
◊ ◊ ◊ ◊ ◊ ◊ ◊ ◊

DAILY EXERCISE
[   ]

TODAY I FEEL

ADDITIONAL NOTES
(Thoughts, Reflections)

DATE _____

S M T W T F S

THINGS I'M GRATEFUL FOR

1. _____

2. _____

3. _____

VITALS

WEIGHT	BLOOD PRESSURE	HEART RATE

TODAYS EVENTS

_____
_____
_____
_____
_____
_____
_____
_____
_____
_____
_____
_____
_____
_____
_____
_____
_____
_____

TODAY GOALS

☐ _____
☐ _____
☐ _____
☐ _____

TASK AND NOTES

....
....
....
....
....
....
....
....
....
....
....
....
....

TODAYS WINS

....
....
....

MY LOCATION

TODAYS LESSONS

....
....
....

MEAL

Breakfast   Lunch

Dinner   Snack

WATER INTAKE

DAILY EXERCISE

TODAY I FEEL

ADDITIONAL NOTES
(Thoughts, Reflections)

DATE ⬭ Ⓢ Ⓜ Ⓣ Ⓦ Ⓣ Ⓕ Ⓢ

THINGS I'M GRATEFUL FOR

1. _____
2. _____
3. _____

VITALS

WEIGHT	BLOOD PRESSURE	HEART RATE

TODAYS EVENTS

_____
_____
_____
_____
_____
_____
_____
_____
_____
_____
_____
_____
_____
_____
_____
_____

TODAY GOALS

☐ _____
☐ _____
☐ _____
☐ _____

TASK AND NOTES

....
....
....
....
....
....
....
....
....
....
....
....
....
....

TODAYS WINS

....
....
....

TODAYS LESSONS

....
....
....

MY LOCATION

MEAL

Breakfast   Lunch

Dinner   Snack

WATER INTAKE
◇◇◇◇◇◇◇

DAILY EXERCISE
[   ]

TODAY I FEEL   😊 😌 😲 😠 🙁

ADDITIONAL NOTES
(Thoughts, Reflections)

DATE (_____)

(S) (M) (T) (W) (T) (F) (S)

THINGS I'M GRATEFUL FOR

1. _____
2. _____
3. _____

VITALS

WEIGHT	BLOOD PRESSURE	HEART RATE

TODAYS EVENTS

_____
_____
_____
_____
_____
_____
_____
_____
_____
_____
_____
_____
_____
_____
_____
_____
_____
_____
_____

TODAY GOALS

☐ _____
☐ _____
☐ _____
☐ _____

TASK AND NOTES

....
....
....
....
....
....
....
....
....
....
....
....
....
....

TODAYS WINS

....
....
....

TODAYS LESSONS

....
....
....

MY LOCATION

MEAL

Breakfast   Lunch

Dinner   Snack

WATER INTAKE
◇◇◇◇◇◇◇◇

DAILY EXERCISE

TODAY I FEEL

ADDITIONAL NOTES
(Thoughts, Reflections)

DATE

(S) (M) (T) (W) (T) (F) (S)

THINGS I'M GRATEFUL FOR

1.

2.

3.

VITALS

WEIGHT	BLOOD PRESSURE	HEART RATE

TODAYS EVENTS

TODAY GOALS

- [ ] _____
- [ ] _____
- [ ] _____
- [ ] _____

TASK AND NOTES

TODAYS WINS

MY LOCATION

MEAL

Breakfast   Lunch

Dinner   Snack

TODAYS LESSONS

WATER INTAKE
◇ ◇ ◇ ◇ ◇ ◇ ◇

DAILY EXERCISE

TODAY I FEEL

ADDITIONAL NOTES
(Thoughts, Reflections)

DATE ( )   (S) (M) (T) (W) (T) (F) (S)

THINGS I'M GRATEFUL FOR

1. _____
2. _____
3. _____

VITALS

WEIGHT	BLOOD PRESSURE	HEART RATE

TODAYS EVENTS

_____
_____
_____
_____
_____
_____
_____
_____
_____
_____
_____
_____
_____
_____
_____
_____
_____
_____
_____
_____
_____

TODAY GOALS

☐ _____
☐ _____
☐ _____
☐ _____

TASK AND NOTES

....
....
....
....
....
....
....
....
....
....
....

TODAYS WINS

....
....
....

TODAYS LESSONS

....
....
....

MY LOCATION

MEAL

Breakfast   Lunch

Dinner   Snack

WATER INTAKE

◊◊◊◊◊◊◊◊

DAILY EXERCISE

TODAY I FEEL   😊 😌 😐 😣 🙁

ADDITIONAL NOTES

(Thoughts, Reflections)

DATE

S M T W T F S

THINGS I'M GRATEFUL FOR

1.
2.
3.

VITALS

WEIGHT	BLOOD PRESSURE	HEART RATE

TODAYS EVENTS

TODAY GOALS

- [ ]
- [ ]
- [ ]
- [ ]

TASK AND NOTES

TODAYS WINS

TODAYS LESSONS

MY LOCATION

MEAL

Breakfast   Lunch

Dinner   Snack

WATER INTAKE

DAILY EXERCISE

TODAY I FEEL

ADDITIONAL NOTES
(Thoughts, Reflections)

DATE

THINGS I'M GRATEFUL FOR

1. _____
2. _____
3. _____

VITALS

WEIGHT	BLOOD PRESSURE	HEART RATE

TODAYS EVENTS

_____
_____
_____
_____
_____
_____
_____
_____
_____
_____
_____
_____
_____
_____
_____
_____
_____
_____
_____
_____
_____
_____
_____

TODAY GOALS

- [ ] _____
- [ ] _____
- [ ] _____
- [ ] _____

TASK AND NOTES

....
....
....
....
....
....
....
....
....
....
....
....
....
....

TODAYS WINS

....
....
....

TODAYS LESSONS

....
....
....

MY LOCATION

_____

MEAL

Breakfast	Lunch
Dinner	Snack

WATER INTAKE

DAILY EXERCISE

TODAY I FEEL

ADDITIONAL NOTES
(Thoughts, Reflections)

DATE ( )

THINGS I'M GRATEFUL FOR

1.

2.

3.

VITALS

WEIGHT	BLOOD PRESSURE	HEART RATE

TODAYS EVENTS

TODAY GOALS

- [ ]
- [ ]
- [ ]
- [ ]

TASK AND NOTES

TODAYS WINS

MY LOCATION

TODAYS LESSONS

MEAL

Breakfast   Lunch

Dinner   Snack

WATER INTAKE
⬠⬠⬠⬠⬠⬠⬠⬠

DAILY EXERCISE

TODAY I FEEL   😊   😌   😐   😠   🙁

ADDITIONAL NOTES

(Thoughts, Reflections)

DATE ( )   (S)(M)(T)(W)(T)(F)(S)

THINGS I'M GRATEFUL FOR

1. _____

2. _____

3. _____

VITALS

WEIGHT	BLOOD PRESSURE	HEART RATE

TODAYS EVENTS

_____
_____
_____
_____
_____
_____
_____
_____
_____
_____
_____
_____
_____
_____
_____
_____
_____
_____

TODAY GOALS

- [ ] _____
- [ ] _____
- [ ] _____
- [ ] _____

TASK AND NOTES

....
....
....
....
....
....
....
....
....
....
....
....
....

TODAYS WINS

....
....
....

MY LOCATION

_____

MEAL

Breakfast   Lunch

Dinner   Snack

TODAYS LESSONS

....
....
....

WATER INTAKE
◊ ◊ ◊ ◊ ◊ ◊ ◊ ◊

DAILY EXERCISE
[   ]

TODAY I FEEL   😊 😌 😵 😠 😖

ADDITIONAL NOTES

(Thoughts, Reflections)

DATE

THINGS I'M GRATEFUL FOR

1. _____
2. _____
3. _____

VITALS

WEIGHT	BLOOD PRESSURE	HEART RATE

TODAYS EVENTS

_____
_____
_____
_____
_____
_____
_____
_____
_____
_____
_____
_____
_____
_____
_____
_____
_____
_____
_____
_____
_____
_____
_____

TODAY GOALS

- ☐ _____
- ☐ _____
- ☐ _____
- ☐ _____

TASK AND NOTES

....
....
....
....
....
....
....
....
....
....
....
....

TODAYS WINS

....
....
....

MY LOCATION

_____

TODAYS LESSONS

....
....
....

MEAL

Breakfast | Lunch
Dinner | Snack

WATER INTAKE

DAILY EXERCISE

TODAY I FEEL

ADDITIONAL NOTES
(Thoughts, Reflections)

DATE

THINGS I'M GRATEFUL FOR

1. _____
2. _____
3. _____

VITALS

WEIGHT	BLOOD PRESSURE	HEART RATE

TODAYS EVENTS

_____
_____
_____
_____
_____
_____
_____
_____
_____
_____
_____
_____
_____
_____
_____
_____
_____
_____
_____
_____
_____
_____
_____
_____

TODAY GOALS

☐ _____
☐ _____
☐ _____
☐ _____

TASK AND NOTES

....
....
....
....
....
....
....
....
....
....
....
....
....

TODAYS WINS

....
....
....

MY LOCATION

_____

TODAYS LESSONS

....
....
....

MEAL

Breakfast   Lunch

Dinner   Snack

WATER INTAKE

DAILY EXERCISE

TODAY I FEEL

ADDITIONAL NOTES
(Thoughts, Reflections)

DATE ⬭

THINGS I'M GRATEFUL FOR

1. _____
2. _____
3. _____

VITALS

WEIGHT	BLOOD PRESSURE	HEART RATE

TODAYS EVENTS

_____
_____
_____
_____
_____
_____
_____
_____
_____
_____
_____
_____
_____
_____
_____
_____
_____
_____

TODAY GOALS

☐ _____
☐ _____
☐ _____
☐ _____

TASK AND NOTES

....
....
....
....
....
....
....
....
....
....
....
....

TODAYS WINS

....
....
....

MY LOCATION

TODAYS LESSONS

....
....
....

MEAL

Breakfast   Lunch

Dinner   Snack

WATER INTAKE
◇◇◇◇◇◇◇◇

DAILY EXERCISE

TODAY I FEEL

ADDITIONAL NOTES
(Thoughts, Reflections)

DATE ⬭   Ⓢ Ⓜ Ⓣ Ⓦ Ⓣ Ⓕ Ⓢ

THINGS I'M GRATEFUL FOR

1. _____
2. _____
3. _____

VITALS

WEIGHT	BLOOD PRESSURE	HEART RATE

TODAYS EVENTS

_____
_____
_____
_____
_____
_____
_____
_____
_____
_____
_____
_____
_____
_____
_____
_____
_____
_____
_____
_____

TODAY GOALS

☐ _____
☐ _____
☐ _____
☐ _____

TASK AND NOTES

....
....
....
....
....
....
....
....
....
....
....
....
....
....

TODAYS WINS

....
....
....

TODAYS LESSONS

....
....
....

MY LOCATION

_____

MEAL

Breakfast	Lunch
Dinner	Snack

WATER INTAKE
◊ ◊ ◊ ◊ ◊ ◊ ◊ ◊

DAILY EXERCISE
[   ]

TODAY I FEEL

DATE ⬭ ⓈⓂⓉⓌⓉⒻⓈ

THINGS I'M GRATEFUL FOR

1. _____
2. _____
3. _____

VITALS

WEIGHT	BLOOD PRESSURE	HEART RATE

TODAYS EVENTS

_____
_____
_____
_____
_____
_____
_____
_____
_____
_____
_____
_____
_____
_____
_____
_____
_____

TODAY GOALS

☐ _____
☐ _____
☐ _____
☐ _____

TASK AND NOTES

....
....
....
....
....
....
....
....
....
....
....
....

TODAYS WINS

....
....
....

TODAYS LESSONS

....
....
....

MY LOCATION

_____

MEAL

Breakfast | Lunch

Dinner | Snack

WATER INTAKE

DAILY EXERCISE

TODAY I FEEL

ADDITIONAL NOTES

(Thoughts, Reflections)

DATE _____  S M T W T F S

THINGS I'M GRATEFUL FOR

1. _____
2. _____
3. _____

VITALS

WEIGHT	BLOOD PRESSURE	HEART RATE

TODAYS EVENTS

_____
_____
_____
_____
_____
_____
_____
_____
_____
_____
_____
_____
_____
_____
_____
_____
_____
_____
_____

TODAY GOALS

- ☐ _____
- ☐ _____
- ☐ _____
- ☐ _____

TASK AND NOTES

....
....
....
....
....
....
....
....
....
....
....
....

TODAYS WINS

....
....
....

MY LOCATION

MEAL

Breakfast .... Lunch

Dinner .... Snack

TODAYS LESSONS

....
....
....

WATER INTAKE

DAILY EXERCISE
[ ]

TODAY I FEEL

ADDITIONAL NOTES
(Thoughts, Reflections)

Visit Us Online

https://pantheria.store

a Find our Books on Amazon

▶ Pantheria

@Pantheria.lofi

@Pantheria.lofi

Made in the USA
Columbia, SC
22 November 2022

71409669R00070